HIGH-TECH

Nanotechnology

Cover: Scientists are studying how nanotechnology could make it possible to put tiny, helpful machines into the bloodstream.

Norwood House Press
P.O. Box 316598
Chicago, Illinois 60631

For information regarding Norwood House Press, please visit our website at:
www.norwoodhousepress.com or call 866-565-2900.

PHOTO CREDITS: Cover: © nobeastsofierce/Shutterstock Images; © BravissimoS/Shutterstock Images, 19; © Brian Kersey/AP Images, 27; © cosinart/iStockphoto, 36; © Dimarion/Shutterstock Images, 25; © Felix Kästle/picture-alliance/dpa/AP Images, 42; © Grand Warszawski/Shutterstock Images, 29; © HO/AP Images, 24; © JPL-Caltech/University of Arizona/University of Neuchatel/ NASA, 35; © last salmon man/Shutterstock Images, 13; © Lightspring/Shutterstock Images, 21; © Mark Herreid/Shutterstock Images, 17; © Moreno Soppelsa/Shutterstock Images, 11; © NASA/JPL, 32; © Niall Carson/Press Association/PA Wire URN:8757515/ AP Images, 8; © Paul Sakuma/AP Images, 5, 38; © plenoy m/Shutterstock Images, 6; © Vadim Sadovski/Shutterstock Images, 40; © Volodymyr Horbovyy/Shutterstock Images, 15

Content Consultant: Alexander Mukasyan, Professor of Chemical Engineering, University of Notre Dame

Hardcover ISBN: 978-1-59953-936-2
Paperback ISBN: 978-1-68404-215-9

Library of Congress Cataloging-in-Publication Data

Names: Kulz, George Anthony, author.
Title: Nanotechnology / by George Anthony Kulz.
Description: Chicago, Illinois : Norwood House Press, [2018] | Series: Tech
    bytes. High-tech | Includes bibliographical references and index.
Identifiers: LCCN 2018004394 (print) | LCCN 2018011782 (ebook) | ISBN
    9781684042203 (ebook) | ISBN 9781599539362 (hardcover : alk. paper) | ISBN
    9781684042159 (pbk. : alk. paper)
Subjects: LCSH: Nanotechnology--Juvenile literature.
Classification: LCC T174.7 (ebook) | LCC T174.7 .K775 2018 (print) | DDC
    620/.5--dc23
LC record available at https://lccn.loc.gov/2018004394

312N—072018
Manufactured in the United States of America in North Mankato, Minnesota.

CONTENTS

Note: Words that are **bolded** in the text are defined in the glossary.

CHAPTER 1

The History of Nanotechnology

In 2013, an animated video appeared on YouTube. It was a 60-second movie called *A Boy and His Atom*. It showed the adventures that two characters had together. The animation was fairly basic. But in some ways, it was the most advanced movie ever made. It even made it into *The Guinness Book of World Records*. What was so special about this movie?

A Boy and His Atom was the world's smallest movie. The width of the original movie, before it was magnified to put on YouTube, was only 50 atoms wide. How did someone make a movie this small?

The World's Smallest Movie

Artists did not draw pictures with a pen to bring *A Boy and His Atom* to life. They did not even use a computer. They used a specialized type of engineering called **nanotechnology**. Scientists made the movie in a lab owned by the technology company IBM. They used a **scanning tunneling microscope** (STM). This device looks at and moves atoms and molecules.

Atoms and molecules make up all things in the universe. An atom is the smallest particle of an **element** that can exist alone. A molecule is a group of one or more atoms that make up a substance. Hydrogen and oxygen are examples of elements. When you combine two atoms of hydrogen and one atom of oxygen, you get one molecule of a substance: water. Atoms cannot be seen by the naked eye. They cannot be seen through an ordinary

Researcher R. Stanley Williams stands with an STM at a laboratory in Palo Alto, California.

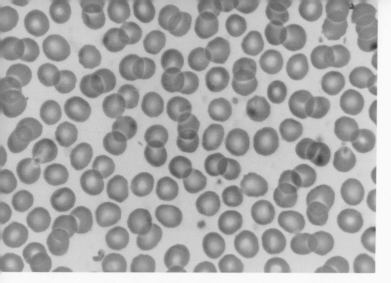

Every red blood cell like the ones pictured here is approximately 10,000 nanometers wide.

make a moving picture. *A Boy and His Atom* used 242 frames. The scientists moved molecules around to make each frame. They used the STM to do so. This short film is just one amazing example of what is possible using nanotechnology.

What Is Nanotechnology?

Nanotechnology is the engineering of very tiny structures. These objects are so small, they are measured in nanometers. A nanometer is one billionth of a meter. The structures are called nanoparticles. Nanoparticles are objects between 1 and 100 nanometers in size. Nanotechnologists use nanoparticles to build a wide range of useful things.

desktop microscope. Scientists must use special microscopes such as STMs.

The scientists filmed *A Boy and His Atom* as a stop-motion movie. In stop-motion movies, artists draw one frame of a scene. Then they create another frame where something is changed ever so slightly. When all the frames of the movie are played one after another rapidly, they

How small is a nanometer? A human red blood cell is 10,000 nanometers across. One strand of human hair is approximately 80,000 nanometers wide. A sheet of paper is 100,000 nanometers thick.

All these objects are too big to be nanoparticles. So, what does exist at that scale? A single atom of the element carbon is approximately one fifth of a nanometer wide. This is too small to be a nanoparticle. But carbon atoms can be grouped together to form a molecule called a nanotube. A nanotube can be as small as one nanometer wide.

Early Explorations in Nanotechnology

The history of nanotechnology starts in the 1950s. In 1959, American physicist Richard Feynman gave a talk called "There's Plenty of Room at the Bottom." The title referred to Feynman's vision for developing technology at an amazingly small scale. He discussed using tiny

DID YOU KNOW?

In 2007, Canadian researchers created a 30-page illustrated book called *Teeny Ted from Turnip Town* with pages 0.07 by 0.10 millimeters in size and text with a line width of 40 nanometers. It can only be read using a microscope.

TEM is the most powerful electron microscope.

particles to help people. He talked about using atoms as building blocks to make objects. Tiny machines would move the atoms into place. Larger machines would control these tiny machines. People would operate the larger machines. He also had ideas on how to pack a lot of information into those tiny particles.

Twenty-eight years before Feynman's speech, Max Knoll and Ernst Ruska invented the transmission **electron** microscope (TEM). It allowed scientists to study atoms and other very small structures. Over the next 50 years, TEM technology got better and better. In 1986, Ruska won the Nobel Prize in Physics for his work on the TEM.

In the late 1970s, American engineer K. Eric Drexler developed the idea of

Ancient Nanotechnology

Scientists developed the idea of nanotechnology in 1959. But nanoparticles have always existed. Ancient people unknowingly used nanoparticles to their advantage. The earliest evidence has been found in Syria. Steel swords forged in 900 CE had multi-walled carbon nanotubes inside them. Tiny wires formed inside the nanotubes. They were a mix of iron and carbon. The nanotubes inside the swords made them very strong. Scientists are still learning how the ancient steel-making process created the nanotubes.

molecular nanotechnology. He based his idea on Feynman's talk. Drexler published *Engines of Creation* in 1986. He wrote about tiny robots, or nanobots, building things with atoms. The nanobots would take atoms from the world around them. People would not control them. They would work all on their own. They would even be able to make copies of themselves.

DID YOU KNOW?

Advanced 3-D printers can print nano-sized materials to build miniature batteries, robots, and even living **tissue**.

Up to that point, however, these were just ideas. The technology did not exist to be able to do these amazing things. But scientists were working on these ideas. In 1981, Gerd Binnig and Heinrich Rohrer built the first STM. This invention enabled scientists to view atoms. The STM has a tip that is only a couple of atoms wide. Scientists apply electricity to the tip. Then they analyze how the electrical charge changes. The changes determine what atoms are next to the tip. In 1989, another IBM scientist, Don Eigler, discovered he could use this device to push atoms around.

In 1982, scientists invented the atomic force microscope (AFM). Binnig developed the microscope with Calvin Quate and Christoph Gerber. The AFM is much more precise than the STM. The tip is less than a nanometer wide. It uses a laser beam to look at and move atoms in three dimensions. Nanotechnologists still use the AFM today. They also use the TEM. It can magnify features as small as 0.2 nanometers.

Why Nanotechnology?

Nanotechnology has become an important part of daily life. People encounter

? DID YOU KNOW?

Under an STM, Eigler moved xenon atoms around on a plate of nickel to spell *IBM.*

some form of it every day. Health care, electronics, architecture, and even space exploration use nanotechnology. It is changing the way humans interact with their environments.

Nanotechnology is changing the medical world. Doctors and nurses use it to learn more about the human body and how it works. They find new ways of giving medicine to patients with

Nanotechnology research is carried out in clean, carefully controlled facilities.

Adding Nanoparticles to Fabrics

Nanoparticles can be very useful when added to fabric. They can help fabrics repel water and dirt. To add nanotechnology to fabrics, scientists add an electrical charge to the fabric fibers. Then they soak the fabric in a liquid that contains nanoparticles. The fibers and nanoparticles have opposite electrical charges. This causes the nanoparticles to bond with the fibers. The fabric is now a new material. It has the properties of the original fibers and the nanoparticles.

nanotechnology. The tiny technology helps create artificial limbs for people. It is also used to monitor a person's health from within the body.

Nanotechnology is improving electronic devices, too. Devices have become much smaller. Technologies people use every day are more portable. Computers are more powerful because more electronics can fit into smaller spaces. All these new products are cheaper to make, so they are cheaper to buy.

Architects can make better buildings with nanotechnology. Buildings are more efficient and durable. Nanotechnology improves insulation that keeps buildings

Nanoparticles help repel water off raincoat fabrics.

comfortable. It makes solar panels more efficient. These improvements also make buildings cheaper to build and own.

Finally, nanotechnology innovations are transforming space exploration. Materials for spacecraft are much lighter and more durable with nanotechnology materials. Advances in rocket development provide better ways to get people into space. Adding nanotechnology to fabric fibers protects astronauts from the harsh conditions of space.

These are just a few of the ways in which nanotechnology is already making a difference in our world. These developments are only the beginning. The future of nanotechnology is just as exciting. But nanotechnologists will have to overcome some challenges for it to reach its true potential.

CHAPTER 2

The Trouble with Nanotechnology

Nanotechnology can improve people's lives. Health care, electronics, architecture, and space applications are some areas in which it can help. But the tiny technology has many other uses. Nanoparticles remove harmful bacteria from the food and water people buy at the supermarket. People can buy shirts and pants that contain nanoparticles that repel water and dirt. Nanoparticles can make a fabric wrinkle-free. It is easy to see that these uses can be a huge benefit to society.

However, nanotechnologists face several challenges. Working with nanoparticles can be difficult. Scientists still have a lot to learn about how tiny particles behave. Others debate who should have access to nanotechnology. Some experts question the possible negative effects of modifying foods or putting nanoparticles into someone's body. Finally, some people think nanotechnology is a bad thing. Much of this fear has been caused by science-fiction movies and books. But some scientists have warned about the possible dangers of nanotechnology.

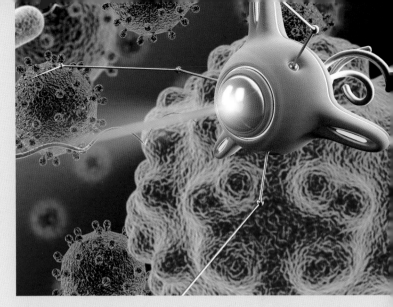

Some people fear nanorobots may cause more harm than good.

Funky Physics

All objects follow the law of gravity. Gravity is the force that pulls everything down to the surface of Earth. This is because Earth has a large **mass**. Smaller objects are attracted to Earth.

People know how gravity affects manufacturing processes at everyday sizes. Workers in factories can weave threads together to make larger products such as blankets and clothing. They can mold and shape metal to make the bodies of cars and trucks.

But working with tiny particles is different than working with large objects. Gravity has less of an effect at this level. Instead, tiny particles are ruled by quantum mechanics. Quantum mechanics is a set of laws that affect atoms and the tiny particles that make them up. It is used to explain forces that act on tiny particles. Electromagnetism and nuclear forces are two of those forces. Quantum mechanics is a relatively new field. It has only been studied for approximately 100 years. Scientists today are still learning how the laws of quantum mechanics work. As they learn more about quantum mechanics, other scientists will develop new nanotechnologies.

The effects of electricity, magnetism, light, and heat change based on an object's surface area. Surface area is the amount of space on the outside of an object. A large number of tiny objects can have a surprisingly large total surface area. A one cubic centimeter block has six sides. If each side is one square centimeter, the surface area is six square centimeters. What if the block was cut into cubes of one cubic nanometer? The total surface area becomes 6,000 square *meters*. This is larger than the surface area of a football field!

Having more surface area is useful. Nanoparticles can be blended into chemicals to make them work better. Chemicals called catalysts are used to reduce toxicity in gasoline fumes. Adding nanoparticles to a catalyst gives the chemical more surface area. It makes contact with and traps more harmful particles in the gasoline fumes. The fumes that are released into the air are cleaner and safer.

Nanotechnology Negatives

Nanoparticles are in many products that people use, including paint and sunscreen. Because nanoparticles are so small, they

A cubic centimeter divided into nanometer blocks has a total surface area greater than that of this entire football field.

Gold in the Nano World

Gold is easy to identify. It has a yellow, shiny surface. It does not rust. This is because it does not bond easily with other materials. However, gold is much different on the nanoscale. Gold nanoparticles absorb light differently. Gold nanoparticles that are 90 nanometers wide absorb red and yellow light, making them look blue or green. At 30 nanometers, they absorb blue and green light, making them look red. Also, gold nanoparticles have more exposed atoms at the corners. They easily bond to other materials. Materials combined with gold can be made much stronger.

can easily get into a person's skin, eyes, and nose. Scientists are studying the effects nanoparticles may have on human health. Some studies have shown some of these particles can be harmful to rats. Scientists believe particle size, shape, and surface area may be factors.

Nanotechnology can also be used to hurt people. Countries are developing ways to use nanoparticles in warfare. Nanoparticles can be used to attack people's bodies. They can even be used to make small nuclear weapons. These would not be as powerful as large weapons. However, they are much easier to make. They would still cause a lot of damage and loss of life. Tiny drones with tiny cameras can be used to spy on

Developing nanotechnology, such as that found in this camera, is still expensive.

people. They can also be used to attack people. These drones could be designed to be so small that no one would be able to see them coming.

Another significant nanotechnology challenge is that it is expensive. Currently, few scientists work in nanotechnology. Some health-related nanotechnology

The Blood-Brain Barrier

The human brain has a way to block harmful chemicals from getting inside. It is called the blood-brain barrier. However, nanoparticles are so small they can go right through the barrier. Some nanoparticles are toxic to the brain. Care must be taken when making them. But because nanoparticles can pass through, scientists can also use this trait to their advantage. These tiny particles could deliver treatments that other medicines cannot.

is available. But it costs a lot of money to develop. Some health insurance companies do not pay for its use. What if only the wealthy could afford these treatments? What about everyone else? In the future, household 3-D printers may be able to print objects at the nano level. If every household had one of these printers, people could just make what they wanted. This would be a bad thing for manufacturers. Many companies would go out of business.

Perceptions of Nanotechnology

Some people are afraid of nanotechnology. Most people do not understand what it is. They do not know what can and cannot be done with nanotechnology. Much of this fear comes from movies and books. They

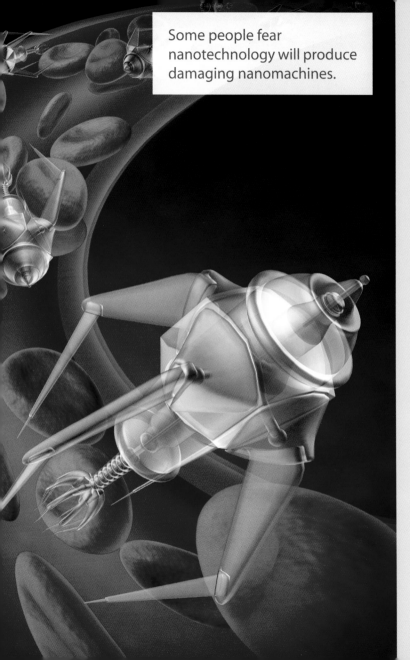

Some people fear nanotechnology will produce damaging nanomachines.

DID YOU KNOW?

The United Nations has a group to handle nanotechnology. This group talks about safe ways to use it. They also offer training and information to the public.

are filled with stories of nanotechnology causing damage and destruction. Characters build tiny weapons. In some stories, it is even used for mind control. Most of these stories do not show realistic risks of nanotechnology.

DID YOU KNOW?

According to *Engines of Creation*, nanomachines would not take long to use up all the material on Earth. If each one copied itself every 15 minutes, it would take less than 48 hours!

However, some scientists have also warned about potential dangers. Drexler talked about this issue in *Engines of Creation*. He imagined nanomachines building any object atom by atom. These nanomachines would take material from the world around them. They would also know how to build copies of themselves. The more nanomachines there are, the faster they could make objects people want. Drexler said nanomachines could continue to make copies of themselves without stopping. All material in our world would eventually be taken, including material that makes up all the people on the planet. There would be nothing left but countless copies of nanomachines. Drexler has since changed his mind about this. He thinks these types of self-copying nanomachines would be too complicated to be useful. The worry about nanomachines eating up everything on the planet is now seen as unrealistic.

CHAPTER 3

Nanotechnology in Everyday Life

Because nanotechnology is small, people often do not notice it. But they do notice technology is changing rapidly. And much of that change is due to nanotechnology.

Many early predictions of nanotechnologists have come true. Feynman predicted computer parts would be made smaller. Computers once required an entire room, but now they fit in a pants pocket. He imagined people could swallow tiny surgical nanotechnology. They would find problems in the body and fix them. Nanotechnology is beginning to do just that. He imagined scientists could build anything from the atomic level up.

Drexler took Feynman's predictions one step further. He predicted nanomachines could fix someone's **DNA**. Nanomachines would detect

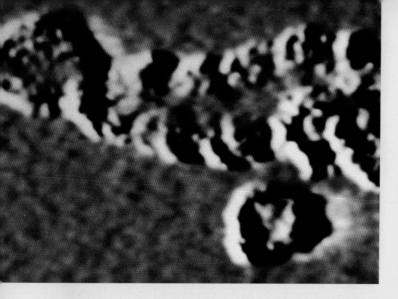

The DNA molecule as seen by an STM

DNA that was not healthy and fix it. He also predicted carbon atoms could be combined with other larger materials. These materials would be super strong. They would make spacecraft and space suits lighter and stronger. Like Feynman, Drexler predicted computer parts would be built on a nanoscale. Computers would then be smaller, faster, and more powerful.

Did Feynman's and Drexler's predictions become reality? Some of the amazing things they predicted are being done today. Others have yet to be accomplished. But scientists are close to making them a reality.

Nanotechnology and Medicine

Feynman and Drexler both predicted nanobots could be placed inside the body to fight disease. Doctors and nanotechnologists are working on this

DID YOU KNOW?

The human body is full of natural nanotechnology. A strand of DNA is two nanometers wide. It contains instructions on how to build everything in the body.

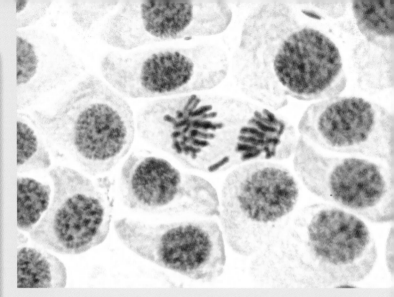

Nanotechnology may help doctors find and eliminate cancer cells (center).

technology. Much of the focus has been on destroying cancer cells.

Cancer is a disease that damages **RNA**. *RNA* stands for ribonucleic acid. RNA does many things in a cell. One of its jobs is to deliver instructions from DNA to cells. The cells follow the instructions and make proteins the body needs. If RNA works properly, proteins are created correctly. The body remains healthy. However, if cancer affects RNA, then the body creates unhealthy proteins instead.

Nanotechnology can fix RNA problems. Scientists have built nanoparticles that look for bad RNA. The nanoparticles are put into the bloodstream. When they

Finding Disease

Quantum dots are special nanoparticles. They give off a particular color when light shines on them. Doctors send them into the body. They are paired up with other nanoparticles that seek out problems in the body. When the nanoparticles find a problem, they attach themselves to it. Ultraviolet light can be used to find where they are. Quantum dots also glow different colors based on how many are grouped together. The color tells how large the problem area is in the body. Quantum dots can also carry treatments for diseases.

find bad RNA, the nanoparticles enter the affected cell. They attach themselves to the bad RNA. By doing this, bad information is no longer sent to the rest of the cells.

Nanotechnology and Electronics

Nanotechnology has created smaller but more powerful electronic devices. Computer displays are clearer. Memory and computer chips are smaller but hold a lot more information. These new technologies use much less electricity.

Engineers can develop smaller computer parts with nanolithography. Nanolithography involves writing a pattern on a surface, usually a **silicon** wafer. Silicon is a hard crystal used to create parts for electronic devices. It is a

A researcher at Northwestern University uses tweezers to place a sample onto a nanolithography instrument.

semiconductor of electricity. The pattern directs how electricity flows through the wafer. Using nanolithography, billions of transistors can be printed on a single computer chip. A transistor is a device that controls electrical signals in a computer. Having more transistors on a chip makes it operate faster.

There are three common ways to perform nanolithography. The most common method is photolithography. First, engineers coat the chip with a chemical. The chemical hardens when exposed to light. Then engineers shine light through a series of lenses, forming a pattern. The light that comes through hardens the chemical in the exposed areas. Then the engineers wash away the extra unhardened chemical. The second method focuses an electron beam onto the wafer. Engineers move the beam around like a pen. It writes a pattern onto the wafer. The last method is like an AFM. Engineers dip the tiny tip of a nanolithography pen in a special chemical. They draw the pattern onto the wafer. The last two methods are slow. They are usually used when not many wafers are needed.

Nanotechnology enables computer displays to become cheaper, smaller, and more efficient. One new way of making displays uses OLEDs, or organic **light-emitting diodes**. OLEDs give off light when electricity is applied to them. Carbon nanotubes can deliver that electricity. Another way uses QLEDs, or quantum dot light-emitting diodes. QLEDs show their colors when either light or electricity is passed through them. A third way is known as electronic paper. The nanoparticles on a paper-thin material reflect light without using electricity. Another display is called FED, or field electronic display. Inside, tiny nanoscopic guns fire electrons at materials in the display that light up. The components in all these new displays are tiny. They use much less electricity than older displays did.

Scientists are building smaller and more powerful computer chips. They have discovered a way to layer the patterns on top of each other in a single chip. The old way of making memory chips used heat. Heating a chip would destroy whatever was on the lower layer. The new chips use nanotubes instead. Little heat is necessary to build them. The lower layer is not ruined when another layer is placed above it.

Nanotechnology and Architecture

The construction industry is starting to make use of nanotechnology. This use of nanotechnology is still very expensive. Engineers continue to study how nanotechnology could improve construction. In the future, nanotechnology could be added to existing materials to make them better.

One promising technology is improved concrete. Concrete is an excellent building material. It is dependable

? DID YOU KNOW?

Certain combinations of nanoparticles can change a surface from see-through glass to a reflective mirror.

and inexpensive. Concrete has been used for thousands of years. Today, nanotechnology is improving this ancient material. Nanoparticles in concrete act as binders. Binders help concrete bond with other materials. Nanoparticles fill in the tiny holes in concrete. This makes the concrete denser and stronger.

Nanoparticles can also coat window glass. The coating keeps heat from

Nanotechnology enables glass to repel dirt, water, and even heat.

moving through glass. Light can still get through the coating. This helps prevent sunlight from heating up a building too much. Another type of coating stores heat inside the nanoparticles when it is warm. When it is cool, the nanoparticles release the heat into the building. Other nanoparticles repel bacteria, dirt, and water. They keep surfaces clean and dry. Finally, some nanoparticles can add fire protection to buildings.

Nanotechnology is helping drive innovation in the solar power industry, too. Nanoparticles are good at trapping sunlight. Solar panels coated with nanoparticles are better than traditional solar panels. They make more electricity and cost less. Because nanoparticles are so small, they can be layered. Solar panel surfaces are now 3-D. This helps trap even more sunlight and generate more electricity from each panel.

Nanotechnology and Space

Scientists have many ideas about how to use nanotechnology to explore space. They are still working out details for many of them. However, they have come up with some amazing discoveries. One of those discoveries is **aerogels**.

At first, aerogels did not include nanotechnology. Manufacturers removed liquid from a gel and replaced it with a gas. The result was a very **porous** substance. A porous substance has many tiny holes called pores. The pores in aerogels are only a few nanometers wide. This makes aerogels very light.

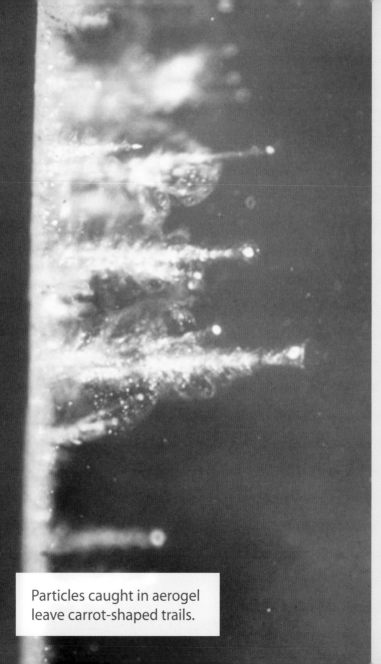

Particles caught in aerogel leave carrot-shaped trails.

Space probes have used aerogels to collect dust particles from comets. The dust particles get trapped in the aerogel. The probes return to Earth, where scientists can study the trapped dust particles. Aerogels have also been used on the Mars Pathfinder mission. The

Nanotechnology in Space

Nanotechnologies have many uses in space exploration. One major benefit is saving weight. Today, spacecraft are very heavy. The space shuttle that carried astronauts and supplies to the International Space Station weighed 165,000 pounds (74,800 kg). But that was when it was empty. Its fuel tank weighed 78,100 pounds (35,4200 kg) empty. Its two rocket boosters weighed 1.83 million pounds (830,000 kg) when fully fueled. Blasting all this weight through the atmosphere and into space is difficult and costly. But nanotechnology could change this. Building materials with nanotechnology are stronger and lighter than conventional spacecraft materials. Engineers are developing new nanotechnology materials to build spaceship hulls and thrusters. Others are developing nanotechnologies for solar sails that could power future spacecraft.

mission sent the *Sojourner* rover to Mars in 1997. It took samples of the ground and snapped pictures. It was coated in aerogels. The aerogels protected the rover from the extreme cold.

Today, scientists use nanotechnology to create aerogels for jobs here on Earth. Carbon nanotubes make aerogels more conductive for electrical uses. Aerogels continue to be good insulators from heat. Scientists hope to use them in electronics. Aerogels are just one example of cutting-edge nanotechnology. What does the future have in store?

CHAPTER 4

01010101010101001010100111001010101010101010101010101010100111001010101010100001C
01010101010101010101010111001010101010100001010101010100101010101010100101010100
1010101010010101010101010101010010101000111001010101010100001010101010101010101

The Future of Nanotechnology

Nanotechnology is used in many different ways today. However, discoveries remain to be made. Scientists are already working on making some of these a reality.

Feynman and Drexler predicted nanomachines would create things at a tiny scale. Feynman thought humans would control these machines using larger machines. The AFM is an example of such a machine. Scientists can control a nanoscopic tip to build things. But this limits what nanotechnology can do.

Drexler's idea was different. Nanomachines would work on their own. They would do their jobs without involving people. Cancer treatments are an example of this. The nanoparticles fight cancer all on their own.

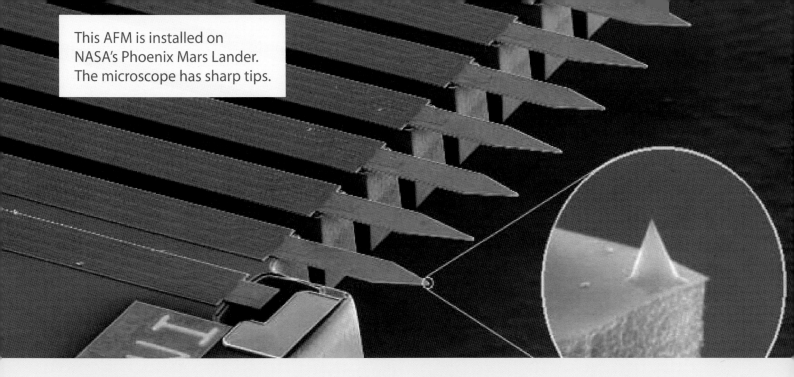

Today, Drexler's vision of nanotechnology is more popular than Feynman's. Regardless, amazing things are being built using nanotechnology. Some of them Feynman and Drexler predicted. Some of them are things neither scientist could have ever imagined.

Advances in Medicine

Medical nanotechnology today only does one thing at a time. Nanotechnology for fighting cancer does only that. But scientists would like it to do more. They would like nanotechnology to monitor different systems in the body and report

An artist's concept of a pill camera that uses nanotechnology

on them. It could also control things in the body that are not working correctly.

Scientists are already making progress. They can place nanosensors on nerve bundles in the body. Nerve bundles are where electrical signals travel from place to place. The signals pass information about the body to the brain. Nanosensors could read these signals and send them to doctors. Someday, these sensors could also make changes to fix problems in the body.

Scientists are researching ways to use nanotechnology to slow aging. As the body ages, some cells stop dividing to form new cells. Other cells may do the opposite. They divide at a fast rate and make too many cells. Scientists are developing a nanotechnology to find

Nanotechnology and Aging

Some products today help with aging. Most focus on the skin. Sunscreens contain nanoparticles that block light. Other products have tiny particles with nutrients inside. The particles help deliver nutrients to the skin to keep it healthy. These products help skin stay young. But scientists are working on ways to keep the entire body young. They are doing tests in labs using rats. Nanocircuitry could replace aging nerves in the brain and nervous system.

these types of cells. Once found, the nanotechnology would either kill them or fix them.

Advances in Electronics

The human brain is more powerful than the most powerful computer. Inside the human brain are neurotransmitters. They are nanoscopic particles that send information from the brain to the rest of the body. Engineers are trying to make computers as powerful as the human brain. One way is to build computers with a structure similar to the brain. The connections in these computers look like neural connections. Engineers use nanoparticles to send information like neurotransmitters do in the human brain. This would make computing much faster and more efficient.

Metal wires 8 to 10 atoms wide may be used in future nanotech medical devices.

Computers could process more information faster with less energy. One group working on this innovation is the US military. Researchers are in the very early stages of understanding this technology. But someday, it may be used to create artificial soldiers and pilots.

With nanotechnology, computers will become smaller and more powerful. They will use less energy. Computers will tackle complex challenges that are out of reach today. Current computer technology is too slow to process complex medical images. These include high-resolution X-rays that look through different layers of the body. Using nanotechnology, computers can copy the way the brain processes this kind of information.

Advances in Architecture

Nanotechnology is being used to build buildings and other structures. Carbon nanotubes and other nanostructures are lightweight yet strong. When combined with other materials, they make those materials lighter and stronger. They can make glass more energy efficient and easier to clean. Insulation with nanotechnologies, including aerogels, keeps houses more comfortable. It helps keep extreme heat and cold out and comfortable air in.

One use for nanotechnology involves putting nanosensors on buildings. Nanosensors could detect molecular weaknesses in a structure. These sensors could alert someone of a possible danger. They could also be used to measure other important things that affect building materials. Temperature, moisture, and vibrations could cause materials to break. Nanotechnology would be useful for critical structures such as bridges, power plants, and aircraft.

Nanotechnology could also take action once a problem has been found. Special nanoparticles could repair found damage. They could go into a problem area and

DID YOU KNOW?

In the future, roads will be built with nanoparticles that repel water, making them last longer.

Space elevators may be made possible by the exceptional strength of nanomaterials.

fill the cracks. Buildings could repair themselves without people. People living inside those buildings would not have to worry about repairs. In fact, those people would never know the building is being fixed around them.

The Future of Space Travel

Drexler predicted building materials would include nanotechnology. He gave an example of building rockets and structures for space exploration. Nanotechnology could also be used to help people travel to space easier. Scientists dream of building a giant space elevator. This elevator would take people from Earth's surface to a station far above Earth's atmosphere. Carbon nanotubes would be used to build ultra-strong cables that could support a vehicle to take people back and forth. Cables with nanotechnology would be much stronger than steel cables alone. They could withstand extreme weather and atmospheric conditions.

Today, space suits are large and bulky. They also get damaged, putting astronauts in danger. Drexler predicted space suits that can shrink to fit an astronaut. He also imagined them being made with nanofibers and nanomachines. The nanofibers would make suits flexible and soft. The nanomachines would repair damage to the suit. They could even convert carbon dioxide molecules the wearer breathes out into oxygen. This would allow astronauts to breathe anywhere without a tank.

Scientists are already designing suits that can shrink to fit the wearer. They have

How to Build a Space Elevator

Sending rockets to the International Space Station is expensive. An elevator to carry things back and forth would be cheaper. But can it be done? First, a large object needs to be put into Earth's orbit. It would rotate along with the planet. Then a cable would attach the object to the ground. The cable would be built using strong nanomaterials. A car would go along the cable from the ground to the object in space. It would run on electricity.

Nanotechnology's future could even include jewelry similar to this Albert Einstein portrait on quartz glass.

developed a nanocomposite material that forms a layer inside the suit. It is known as a **shear-thickening fluid**. The fluid thickens when a sharp force punctures it. If a tiny meteoroid punches a hole in a space suit, this fluid could seal up the hole and protect the wearer.

There are also some space-related uses for nanotechnology that Drexler never dreamed of. Scientists want to use nanosensors to analyze things found on other planets. Nanosensors could help discover if Mars has water or other materials that could help people live there. The nanosensors would be cast over an area of the planet as a large mesh net. The nanosensors would record data about the planet's surface.

Nanotechnology has come a long way since Feynman's famous 1959 lecture. Tiny particles that are invisible to the naked eye are now making a difference in everyday life. Every new technology brings new challenges, and nanotechnology is no different. Scientists are working to overcome these difficulties, making nanotechnology cheaper and safer. As the technology improves and spreads to new areas, it will become an important part of our high-tech modern life.

GLOSSARY

aerogels (AIR-oh-jelz): Gels where the liquid is removed and replaced with a gas.

DNA (DEE EN A): A molecule that contains instructions on how to build everything in a living thing.

electron (eh-LEK-tron): A particle with a negative charge that is smaller than an atom.

element (EL-uh-ment): A fundamental substance that contains only one kind of atom.

light-emitting diodes (LITE-eh-mit-ing DI-odz): Materials that give off light when electricity is applied to them.

mass (MAS): The measure of the amount of material contained in an object.

nanotechnology (na-no-tek-NAWL-uh-gee): The study and creation of structures smaller than 100 nanometers.

porous (POR-is): Having many tiny holes.

RNA (AR EN A): A copy of DNA's instructions a cell uses to create proteins needed for a living thing.

scanning tunneling microscope (SKAN-ing TUN-uhl-ing MI-kro-skope): A device that uses electrical charges to look at and move atoms.

shear-thickening fluid (SHEER-thik-en-ing FLOO-id): A liquid material that turns into a solid when it is struck with a sharp force.

silicon (SIL-uh-kon): An element used in electronics and computers that is a good conductor of electricity.

tissue (TISH-oo): Cells of the same kind that provide structure in the body.

FOR MORE INFORMATION

Books

Jennifer Swanson. *Super Gear: Nanotechnology and Sports Team Up*. Watertown, MA: Charlesbridge, 2016. Discover how nanotechnology helps the world's top athletes.

Lisa J. Amstutz. *Discover Nanotechnology*. Minneapolis, MN: Lerner Publishing Group, 2017. Discover more about the devices that nanotechnologists are developing.

National Geographic Kids. *Science Encyclopedia: Atom Smashing, Food Chemistry, Animals, Space, and More!* Washington, DC: National Geographic, 2016. Learn all about atoms, matter, physics, and future technologies.

Websites

Explain That Stuff: Nanotechnology (www.explainthatstuff.com/nanotechnologyforkids.html) This website includes several examples of everyday objects measured in nanometers.

Nanooze (www.nanooze.org) This website is edited by Carl Batt, a professor at Cornell University. It's all about nanotechnology.

Nanozone (www.nanozone.org) This website has interactive games to help you discover more about nanotechnology.

YouTube: A Boy and His Atom (https://youtu.be/oSCX78-8-q0) Watch the video that made it into the Guinness Book of World Records.

INDEX

Q

Quantum dots, 26, 28
Quantum mechanics, 15–16
Quate, Calvin, 10

R

RNA, 25–26
Rohrer, Heinrich, 10
Ruska, Ernst, 8

S

Scanning tunneling microscope
    (STM), 5, 10
Shear-thickening fluid, 43
Silicon wafers, 26
Space elevators, 40–41
Syria, 9

T

Transmission electronic
    microscope (TEM), 8, 10

U

United Nations, 21

George Anthony Kulz holds a master's degree in computer engineering. He is a member of the Society of Children's Book Writers and Illustrators and writes stories and nonfiction for children and adults. He currently lives in Rhode Island with his wife and four children.